the whither poems

Catherine Edward

The Acorn Press
Charlottetown
2019

AC⊕RNPRESS

P.O. Box 22024
Charlottetown, Prince Edward Island
C1A 9J2
acornpresscanada.com

Edited by Dianne Hicks Morrow
Designed by Matt Reid
Printed in Canada

Library and Archives Canada Cataloguing in Publication

Title: The whither poems / Catherine Edward.
Names: Edward, Catherine, author.
Identifiers: Canadiana 20190170425 | ISBN
9781773660363 (softcover)
Subjects: LCSH: Nature—Poetry.
Classification: LCC PS8609.
D78 W58 2019 | DDC C811/.6—dc23

Canada Council   Conseil des Arts
for the Arts   du Canada

The publisher acknowledges the support of the
Government of Canada, the Canada Council of the Arts
and The Province of Prince Edward Island.

For
Michael ~ Gethin ~ Cecily ~ Eric

Table of Contents

I. Whither a footstep fell

That most peculiar feeling. 3

Old poet from somewhere. 4

Dream steps 5

Impossible chance 6

Colouring the day. 7

Being eighty-five. 8

Poems fall like water 9

Smithereens 10

A solitary beat 11

Clutter dream. 12

Key. 14

East to the sea 15

White rose. 16

Voice stilled 17

Between white & black. 18

Times mean measure. 19

Moss gathers a stone 20

Iced rosettes 21

II. Whither the sun shines & the wind blows

Hanging lavender 25

Creamsicle shoes. 26

Change that beckons. 27

Auricle 28

Dragonfly day. 29

Willow snow. 30

Stillness 31

Coffee table sculpture. 32

Cold ending. 33

Divinity fudge and cinnamon toast. 34

Like ice that needn't melt. 35

Near perfect 36

On an April afternoon. 38

One hundred day miracle. 39

Silk magnolias 40

Green fire. 41

III. Whither then we tell

Blue quince. 45

Embroidered garden *for Andrew Marvell*. 46

Falling up. 48

Cyclamen 49

Spider 50

Titus the dandelion uncle. 51

Swallow Heart 53

Words shaped like a pineapple. 55

A round turn & two half hitches 56

Tatted blue 57

Time in a tisket. 58

City planners 60

Sandstone 61

Worms 62

The *Fall of Rome* encore 63

White as a whale. 64

Wolfy. 65

Wrinkled gold 66

IV. Whither are we bound

Now and then, alone 69

Cadence 70

Faraway 71

No food. 72

Echo. 73

Glass sky 74

Leaf paint. 75

Butterfly wind 76

Dry tears 77

Quiet place 78

Night heart 79

Teresa of Avila. 80

Quinquagesima 81

Lark. 82

Window ash 83

If I had a river. 84

Wings 85

Banquet 86

Old perfect poem 87

I. Whither a footstep fell

That most peculiar feeling

That most peculiar feeling
stuck between shoulder blades
no moving without touching
that most peculiar feeling
that goes everywhere
without invitation.

Always cooler in the hollow
where the mist gathers and
where cold air falls neatly.
A relief in high summer to
wander there for blackberries
but chilling in winter
when everything has gone.

That peculiar feeling is cold comfort.
No reason to expect a favour for my heart
which beats as usual and asks
for nothing more.

I cannot know the divers things
that shape a day's unfolding
so wholly devouring
till, gorged on its events
wait for another try, though

there are no blackberries
in the hollow.

Old poet from somewhere

Old book. Old poet from somewhere
in olden times.
He wonders about the colour

blue, like the silky back of a jay,
iridescent in sun
deep under shadow.

I can talk to a blue-jay if I feed it daily.
Tse-tse cheerful, friendly sounds.
It sees me, tips its head in recognition.

Another blue, like the hard blue
of a Bristol Cream bottle
sleek and stately, I toss

it out to sea. It'll be
back in fifty years
scoured into blue treasure.

A child will find it on the shore
take it home in a bucket and
wonder at the sea glass that

is so much like the silky blue of a jay
iridescent in sun
smooth under shadow.

Dream steps

Where are my footsteps before the dawn?
Sheltered in a dream

surrendered in one waking breath
inhaled, exhaled, lost.
Gone.

Can I hold on one more day
perhaps another few
measured animation
my quest, my desire.
Pray.

Daydreaming a familiar trial
place to place, on heel and toe
more brittle than a wish
harder, all the while
            wincing.

I might not mind the chair
were it coloured purple
a sky blue seat, tiny wheels
someone lovely to push it.
            There.

Impossible chance

I walked along a shore where
tide would not change
immutable lame bastion of time
set on a course of no beginning
against another more precise ending
of cannot be, cannot be.

No beginning without an ending.
Not the usual way of tides.

A gossamer strand
hung in a silent forest
threaded a needle
embroidered a leaf where
a blossom should have been.

There were no petal colours
no pink, purple, yellow or red
only rich moss fern green.
A leaf, perchance
would do, would do.

New cloth.
So smooth,
with only a leaf
to show.

Never mourn the un-embroidered flower
an extravagant innocence
of no harsh motive
altered with sweet clemency
into a leaf of matchless grace.

A pure gift without reserve—
saved forever to wash upon
that shore of no return
where tide neither comes nor goes
but is ever the same.
The same.

Colouring the day

Never a sleepyhead, childish waking so simple
movement from dream to morning
there for the painting with energetic colours
no inhibition of wrongly mixing primaries

no sense of me except what I might be
that day, destined to be revealed with
everything unveiled in my colour chase

a red and white tap dancer
white satin, red rick-rack and
those maical tapping shoes

a turquoise trapeze artist hanging—
knowing the danger, pleased to be
given the chance to try so high

brown black capes to set a drama
amongst the craggy rocks, too rough
for anything but children's games

a sundown feeling of many things
shaped as I pleased.
Then came a morning with its

armoured body clench, snatching
my longing to live
the day as if nothing bothered me.

Too soon reveals a new
world where everything asks for
a letting go, even dreaming.

Being eighty-five

Calling out
from a deep somewhere
into the heart of nowhere,
fragmented pieces replace
shadows.

Fantasy has no issue
with reality.

Terror, left by a nightmare
wandered into daylight
devoured memory
left a thousand dreams of
    fallen
      behind
        yesterdays.

Confusion mistook emptiness
for the loss of love.

No refuge in forgetting
He gave angels
charge over you
    and the dragon
    was trampled under
    their feet.

Poems fall like water

I read a poem today
about loss, so sad
like everyone's loss
enough to make one cry.

Next day it spoke
of triumph in the
moment's misery
a view missed before.

From the middle of imagination
from the deep centre of one thought
into a hundred more
poems fall like water.

Last evening there was a poem
waiting on the sky at dusk
no writing fast enough
to capture fading colours
the setting sun unaware.

But colours blaze the imagination
where poets are privileged to see.

Rain falls on a garden
a rose blooms.
A muse drinks
until poet's thought
quenches the thirst.

Smithereens

I dropped a poem
like glass into smithereens

a hard world out there
not for throwing
poems around

didn't throw
dropped it
an accident

I loved that poem

so many shards
in poems
so fragile

don't make glass poems

I must do
for light
to see
though things
like memory

A solitary beat

In the middle chest
a little à la gauche
    settled there
    since forever
marking time, like a
silent fisher, but
      wandering places
of peril, marvel, puzzle
providence to guide

obscure sagas
legends of love
enigmatic allegories
tragic tales
defined in a solitary beat
      as large as the world
      as small as a feathered fly
casting ripples on the water

barely noticed by a fish
yet dazzled by the sun
when evening casts its
final saffron arch
    like a last kiss.

Clutter dream

clutter imposed itself
order misplaced carelessly
a muddled head

tangled thoughts in
a tightly mangled tryst
ideas fancy a clear outline

the mind top-stitched itself
even, tight, unyielding seams
no loosening or it will tear

a strange language when
that tear falls down a cheek
wet and hot with hope

lost in a nightmare's landscape
with frozen feet, no turning left
allowed in swarming city throngs

one lone untangled thought
an ideal curtain to lower
upon a cluttered dream

find that old perfect road
go there again where
fast feet run in high places

but once, only once, for
dreams have no return
however, ever and forever

run from the clutter confusion
from noise with fuchsia lights
and no map anywhere

turn right, right, right, right
devising a resolute left
outwitting a dreamscape,

never before, never since
so I'll stay there
forever.

Key

In a storage place for words
letters dwell in a red velvet box
gilt edged, medallion keyhole.
The key is lost.
No chance of mixing letters
words of melancholy
heartache, sorrow,
The key is lost.
Silence.

One day the top flies open.
A message, closed with sealing wax:
"So you found the key.
The red velvet box is yours.
Mix the letters as you will."
I took my pen and wrote a
dancing line filled with fun.
The heart is found.
Rejoice.

East to the sea

Of all the rememberings and forgettings
that splash like tears on a lily pad
one with robin-like vigour
comes home against the odds
sings a summer song
moves me like a symphony.

Of all the breakings and heavings
that crash like waves along the shore
one with oaken heart
stands tall against the tide
faces a noble gale
moves me like a mountain.

Of all the wonderings and hopings
that grow like stories in a heart
one with serendipity
takes steps along a blind path
finds a painted door
colours me like a rainbow.

Now there are loseings
with star fish and satin wind
moss on my shoes
not a signpost to be seen.
Turn around.
I shall face the sea unknown
though robins fly inland.

White rose

i.

Rose behind my eyes

I saw a white rose:
impossible to sleep
in such a flower's spell,
expectant
a white rose against a black green silence.

That rose imposed itself
upon me all the day
white things:
phlox, baby's breath, clouds
white feelings:
hope, patience, mercy.

I had no eyes for
yellow, red, or blue.

ii.

Darkness fell at last.

I'd wait, look closely.
In the dream I saw again
the white rose behind my eyes
with light passing through white petals
as if etched on glass

a perfect spider's web
weaving silk into a veil
white roses, white background.
held high, in the middle of the night
in the time of black greenness.

I wasn't sure.
I was almost sure.

Voice stilled

voice mute in its box
that will not vibrate
a small flutter
that tries an "oh"
to hear
so quiet

hands held
fold, open, close
no rhyme scribbled
of late, since before
then
so still

muse flickers
tinted flashes
hesitant
fade away
like rainbows
so still, so quiet

Between white & black

In its lowness
somewhere
between white and black
dark and light rests
nothing of itself
after the red hot fire
but cinder shadows
a mezzotint leaden
frown of sky.
Then
a beam breaks
wide-sun-blue
we look up
smile
and carry on
with our day
turned
inside out
by the sky

Times mean measure

words melt like April's ice
create rivulets for letters going back
where they've belonged since before
they were written
more, more, more, and more
many more
not nearly enough when
words give way to thoughts
cherished in time's mean measure
equal, but soon insufficient
though I remember when
they arrived

Moss gathers a stone

Moss mounds like thatch
between rock crannies
progressing slowly, inexorably
like pushing lead thoughts
with no spaces.
Some things are hard
    to move
impenetrable dense twists
that ought to be
    light as a feather
    and as willing to move
    as air floating
sharing green whispers
echoed in colour's constancy.
But chance intervened
a flirt with
time, labour, age,
transforming prospects
and glanced upon some
    things tangible
    perhaps or maybe not,
    one never knows for sure.
I'm growing old watching.

Iced rosettes

(on being a grandmother)

Age regarded a quiet space around its heart
considered its habit - still, with order
where time and space linger lightly
woven as fabric with temperament's
woof and warp intertwined over years

a matter of life's enduring design
strong as tailor's thread
delicate as a moonbeam
precarious as the dawn
where joys and sorrows merge.

Raucous embellishments changed
the above-mentioned design
unexpected, like an extravagant diet full
of champagne and marzipan cakes iced
with rosettes piped upon new life.

Age revised its habit for time and space
drew a deep breath
inhaled the heavenly unimagined
felt joy beating near its heart
then sang.

II. Whither the sun shines & the wind blows

Hanging lavender

Time to harvest my belle lavender
the fragrance of Provence
I travel in an armload of perfume.

It hangs to dry from a pine beam
to make sweet lavender pomanders
full of summer thoughts, tender mornings
with bare feet and coffee on the porch
hummingbird on delphinium.

On the serious side of the season
change is my luminous portion
where summer gives to autumn
a windy circle into winter—
coffee served in a slower dawn
warmth from the fire in the stove

lavender lingers in the linen chest
and I wonder if the hummingbird
is safe in South America.

Creamsicle shoes

dreams melt like creamsicles on hot days
hard to catch drips before they fall
in orange shapes to the ground
never to be picked up again
gooey sticky puddle

creamsicle shoes are for walking
with a touch of whimsy
to give bounce and tenacity
for tying a tight tie
no falling away

so many things for eyes to see then
red rocks, sea air, buttercups
sand, ants, driftwood, mirth
all belonging together in a
creamsicle day

captured in summers glad memory
no drip fallen upon the ground
another perfect day to be "a cow on the Island."

Change that beckons

September blows on a pale grey day
lush greens of summer linger
wind soft and humid
change waits to reveal itself in
the crispness of an apple-breeze

gardening moves
from primping to harvest
disarray takes on satisfaction
comfort in the knowledge
we move on to autumn things

stack firewood
put up pickles
freeze pumpkin
frolic in fallen leaves
clear woods trails

all for winter's inglenook
everything given up
except that final game of croquet
one day in late November's nakedness

Auricle

mist falls in the hollow of my heart
an early morning melancholy
life blood
auricle to auricle
slowed by fruitful, metaphors of autumn leaves
red   brown   gold
dry   blow away
nestle in deep sombre piles
cover reposing flowerbeds
needful of warmth
silent resilience to last the winter
a quiet wait while blood pumps
right auricle   left auricle
right ventricle   left ventricle
even under snow
to prevent an attack of the heart
before summer returns
and roses bloom
again
in the rising morning mist

Dragonfly day

A perfect day to stop
beside the bayberry
on a sunny river bank
and watch the grass closely
to see who might be there.

Ants – brown, black, red –
how hard they work
the only labourers who haul
twice their body weight home
on the chance it might be useful.

Grasshopper on a weed
leapt fifty times his body length
to a far blade of grass
a peculiarly exacting sport.

Tiny dragonfly set
upon the bayberry
russet wings so fragile
a sunbeam turned them
into glistening, burnished copper filigree.

Preposterous that such dainty wings
can lift so portly a carcass
tiny red lipstick dragonfly mouth
eyes, black and beady
a simple, friendly, little face
a child would draw.

Willow snow

If, at once, the willows hang
under leaf and under snow
burdened leaf given no chance
to complete its autumn drift
and many-coloured dance
the snow, come too soon, has
no welcome, nor pretty chance.
Must I rake leaves in snow?

If a heart is heavily bowed
like a willow under snow
is there a song to be sung
while clothed in dismal robe
cold and drearily hung?

Is this a velvet
mantle or an icy rung?

Or a heart's work to lift
that frosty cloak and peel
its willow snow sting
from around a tender core
hear the song it wants to sing
and find a bud there
resting, until spring?

Stillness

No sound, so still in the night
birds gone
No cicada, no crickets, no peepers
no leaves, no blossoms.
November.
All is hushed and cold.

An eclipse of the moon
shrouds brilliance
smooth like mink oil
rubbed on soft leather boots
before the first storm.

A wild wind will blow
savage sounds of snow.
A temper
then softly stilled.

Afterward
time to remember
months warmed by the fire,
a northern comfort offered.

Coffee table sculpture

a plant sculpture
fireweed gone to seed
bare curly willow
germ of liatris
dried wheat
dead things

the fireweed
burst its seed pods
the sculpture
sits robed in unexpected
clouds of fluff
not entirely dead
at all
a seed cloud

a nearly dead explosion

Cold ending

bluest blue jay hurt its wing
huddled behind the wood box
in minus thirty degrees
perhaps to give up though
maybe to huddle

might he
give the bird
a blanket
or bring it in
near the stove
chances
to get through
the night

or
vain human
meddling
that
could kill it
like the cold outside
did

Divinity fudge and cinnamon toast

The wind bit like a bear trap
froze flesh in thirty seconds
never stopped for days on end.

Snow whipped into hard peaks
like divinity fudge
so hard we walked on top.

Most things held fast, but
a savage blast moved snow
like beach sand to the brink

leaving naked earth
to face a naked chill
blowing, wild thin whips

til topsoil primped snowy fields,
like cinnamon toast
sprinkled heavily. Gone cold.

Fall ploughing too late reaps
topsoil for the neighbours
or the ditch and then the river.

Pristine winter gone.
Farmers' dollars crimped
while barely scraping by, they say.

I cannot be the
one to scrape it all up.
Who cares?

Like ice that needn't melt

The love dove returns
in minus thirty degrees
twice a day
or she will starve.
That's some high tech garb she models
to break the bite of wind that blows
snow giants over the fields.

How many little birds
perished in the woods last night?

Coldest in one hundred years
two wood stoves burning
made all our difference.

Twelve weeks ago
I put hyacinths to chill
in a pot of stones
brought them into warmth when
they had burst their bulbs.

A pink blossom and blue opened
yellow and white followed
the fragrance of hyacinth
freely given in the dead of winter
recalls sweet summer air
like clover honey
grass in the morning dew
butterflies in the lilies.

Hyacinth pays no heed to
snow giants or icicles
makes no distinction
between January or July sun
nor shall I.

Near perfect

In spring I dig
in the good red earth
watch swallows fly
pick lily of the valley
and lilac purple & white
fragrances offered as
perfumes from heaven
make bouquets tulip daffodils

In summer I languish
in a green green shade
watch robins grow fat
children in the sprinkler
drink mint tea
eat lavender ice cream
find shells driftwood on the shore
make bonfires under the stars

In autumn I wake
to frosted asparagus fern
mist hiding the river and hills
walk in a scarlet golden wood
gather pumpkin bouquets of
chrysanthemum sedum sage
place quince in a bowl
aroma of paradise in fall

In winter I catch snowflakes
fashion snow angels
ski in a sparkling snowy wood
sit by the fire reading poems
with mulled cider
gingerbread apple butter
while snow giants blow
and snow buntings celebrate

a parade of perfection
on my island
then along comes
the Ides of March and
I wish to go to Tuscany.

On an April afternoon

went out on
an April afternoon
officially spring

wellies and two sticks
like a highland hiker
on a softer path

watched eagles soar
around the tallest pine
setting up house

the ducks
fluttered off the water
and flew away

the last rim of snow cleaved
to the river bank
sun triumphs in the end

yesterday's stubble, fragrance of brindle
today's aroma of awakening soil
tomorrow's perfume of wild clover

signs of spring under
the white cloud eagle tummy
so high up

One hundred day miracle

Wind whorls over the land
while on the ground, snow shells form
winter sculpting by an
ethereal white frozen wind.

I long to know words
in a conch shell
hear only a murmur
though the sea is raging.

a snow shell's song is cold and aloof
muffled phrases for memorizing
before they disappear without a trace
licked up by the sun.

from the time of snow drifts
until the fragrance of lilacs
only one hundred days—
a miracle.

Silk magnolias

Grey, a silent retreat
backdrop for others to take centre stage.

Even November
harbours no thought of up-stage
retiring with generosity, disrobed of colour
undone and uncovered for all to see.
Undressed when wild wind blows cold
unlike summer, fully dressed in sweet warmth.

The shadows of November set a different scene
elaborate filigree on frozen ground
a most unexpected beauty.

In Georgia they pin magnolias on the trees
when full spring does not arrive in time
It was the reason for watching blossoms
with hungry eyes
while trees up North have not yet thought of spring
but wear the nakedness of November—
now tiresome, embarrassing, impatient and stale.

Those pinned-on magnolias spoil the truth of spring.
How like us who cannot wait.

Green fire

As if it wasn't enough already
candles lit on the branch tips of
spruce pine fir hemlock
bright green fire
dessert at the end
of springs feast
filling winter weary northerners
with eye candy of Junes final fling
our last trophy
too many greens to count
while many coloured lupins cavort
in unexpected places

III. Whither then we tell

Blue quince

When there is fruit enough
I shall make quince jam
to eat with a runcible spoon
the one I dreamt of owning
then found in our barn
what luck.

I weeded in the quince this morning
all fallen upon with deepest blue
delphinium petals
blue for resilience
like a new tea.
Blue quince.

It was the very morning
a sad silver-haired woman called me.
I told her about
the blue delphinium petals
on the quince
to cheer her, and yarrow

behind the quince that stood
twined with purple vetch
and red clover three feet high
much too much overtaking
and I never saw the like.

I did not disturb
blue delphinium petals
on fancied quince
and I have my runcible spoon.

Embroidered garden

For *Andrew Marvell*

She slipped in silently
sat upon the blue satin bolster
hands folded, right upon left
awaiting benediction
from someone, somewhere
nowhere to be seen.
It was chilly.

Then, attending morning's
blessing at her window
sun generously hers for awhile
an ephemeral eleven o'clock lamp
she devised a garden of stitches
laid out upon a square of
unbleached evenweave.

At garden's centre, in pearl cotton
a bed of Maltese cross
Pekinese stitches for a hedge
oval beds each corner filled with
checkered chain band, raised chevron
Guilloche, Chinese knot
diamond bullion, threaded herringbone
Armenian edging, all in stranded floss.

An embroidered garden
unearthed within the poem
he left upon that oaken table
its why or how, its hope
its end, unclear.
He'd not confessed
loves oblique intersection
no reason to believe it hers.
He'd gone.

Stitch by artful stitch, she
sowed a matchless formal garden
though, in truth, she sat upon
a seat cast by cold stone walls.

Falling up

Where I was born
it was not flat.
Violet hills rolled down
to meet the eternal grey sea
with the roar of great breakers
upon a rocky headland.

I climbed up
always up
expecting another side
a going down side.

Going down is harder
I discovered on a mountain
toes cram to the front of shoes
falling down is easy
in sheer descent.

A flat ridge with wheat
swelling in the breeze like sea waves
made me lonesome for the shores of home.
But I like gold and stayed a while
in that particular marvel
straight and yellow
against my sea blue temper.
Ever since I've liked yellow and blue together.

Love.
Nothing else
gold and blue.
I came down from the
sea of wheat
and headed home.

Cyclamen

(A Villanelle)

A snow white cyclamen sublime
craved cool breath upon its cheek
like chilblains to this soul of mine.

Then rose artful dawn a gentle clime
and shone its luminous morning sun
on snow white cyclamen sublime.

Up stretched those alba arms so fine
above rich carpet leaves for shielding
chilblains from this soul of mine.

In tepid air it bent a full-bowed rhyme
when came a honey breath too warm for
A snow white cyclamen sublime.

Innocent flower fell before its prime,
warmth debars while cold enchants
a snow white cyclamen sublime,
like chilblains to this soul of mine.

Spider

Spider makes no complaint
about the lonely road it travels
tiny critter on the face of a wall
a vast nothingness——
how can it hope to fashion
anything from a blank state?
It clings there so still,
then moves deftly
drops a gossamer strand
strength of steel

to fashion an
elaborate lace trap.

I cannot do that, instead
stumble under the weight
of life's ordeal
wishing I knew how to find
strength on a thread
though it was given me
so easy to forget
what is stronger than steel.

Meanwhile
a spider makes no weary grimace
no worry, and, no never-mind.

Titus the dandelion uncle

Great Uncle Titus panned for gold up north.
No one knew if he ever found any.
A legal document made the rounds
for all the family to sign
after he died
in LaLoche, Saskatchewan
leaving no will.
It was commonly believed that if we all
pooled this resource there would be enough
after legal fees for a bottle of rum.

Yesterday I came upon a dazzling green field
dressed in a golden frock
shocking on such a grim grey day.
Light skulked from under the clouds
touched down upon that field embellished
in waves of small suns doing
their dandelion dance.

Each dandelion blossom has
a thousand tiny yellow petals.
Children bring bouquets for mum
their eyes full of crinkly love.

Usually they are surprised how quickly
these offerings droop
while mother's surprise is
the simple extravagant resolve to keep
a fresh supply bouqued till there are
no more jars.

One day, dandelions were outlawed.
No more lawns with dandelions.
There can be no respect for neighbours with dandelions.
It is enough to make one move to the country.

I never knew Uncle Titus.
They say he had a love affair with the north
and never was much for practicalities
wife or home or children.
No lawn with dandelions.
He had a backpack, a squeeze box and a pipe.
A pair of boots. A walking stick. A song.
Tall with a grand moustache like handlebars.
Grey mustachios looking for gold.

Here dandelions have the upper hand
sun drops on the fields.
Later will o' wisps appear
a thousand petals to make a thousand
silver grey weightless seed kisses
to blow to the brink of heaven.

Once I bought a paperweight
with a dandelion fluff inside
and gave it away quick as the wind
to cheer a friend.

I imagine Uncle Titus
wandering through a dandelion garden
in his prospector's hat
his wide grey moustache, a smile underneath,
quenched, at last, by the posy of gold in his hand.

I never knew Great Uncle Titus but
I, too, have boots, a walking stick and a song.
And worldly wealth enough for a bottle of rum.

Swallow Heart

a poem got lost
in the heart of a swallow
took it to Rio de Janeiro
where they dance the tango
kept it all winter

I'd forgotten where it was
p'rhaps planted with the
autumn bulbs

come spring
electric blue squill & tiny daffodils
dance a northern tango
and pirouette
a waltz into summer

but no poem there

this morning a swallow emerged
from the barn
arrived last evening
in time again for

warm caresses of summer
beach sand brought home
shells and sand dollars
tiger lilies, cucumbers, parsley
swinging in the hammock
hodgepodge for supper

the barn is yours
till the fledglings can fly
ready for the trip to Rio

another poem sits in
the weeping mulberry
can you make a small detour to
the edge of the world where
swallows deliver poems?

a green, green poem about
a flight from brown to expectation.
& thank you for all the bugs you ate
no mosquitoes all summer

you left so quietly
the air is empty without
your wings, your tail
your soaring for the joy of it

so far to fly   so small   so brave
so many beats in your swallow heart

Words shaped like a pineapple

It was the hat   caught my eye first
so erect with a   flaunt of spikes   leaning off centre
beneath that hat   a prickly corset or
bristly crinoline
I couldn't decide
all so spiny, so untouchable.
First remove the hat without a brim
then, a lateral cut, further incisions
expose that luscious yellow interior.
Juicy is the inside of spiny. Like sad
is the inside of mad. Not what it seems.
Something for the brave. Where are the
predators who will prick a paw, break
a beak? They've left it for hands, fingers
that work together for a feast
called fresh fruit salad.

A round turn & two half hitches

Oars dip in the water
no splash with an edge sliced just so
I am the rower, I am the passenger
and proud.

I lost an oar that day
slipped out of the oarlock
it floated back, to me.
How lucky.

Piddling promise in a rowboat
enough to keep one's bearings
faint chance for getting lost.
Even so, I was.

A round turn & two half hitches
learned on a lanyard in the Girl Guides
the knot to nowhere, wondered how it would
save me if I ever got lost.

I rowed the boat to Tracadie Island
by myself, alone, thinking
preferred no interruptions
just listening with waiting.

For fun I slid down the dunes
swam the sand off me
ate my sandwich, drank lemonade.
Tide came in, told me to go home.

I had a rowboat and no worries
about getting lost or confounded
with my round turn & two half hitches
tied to a memory.

Tatted blue

Holding the thrall of expectation
near the edge of one's heart is
fraught with the dismay Aunt Mary
felt when her tatting went wrong.
The tiniest thread with the thinnest hook
a silky strand spun into
something more amazing than itself.
Hardly seemed possible. Like the tatted collar
on my cornflower blue dress, when I was little
before I could write my name in pencil.

I'd stand very straight, hold my head
just so, knowing there was
something pretty to show off—
tiny puffed sleeves, pearl buttons on
scalloped edging all round my waist.
I loved that dress.
It made me know clouds.

I grew. Mama gave my cloud dress away
without asking, though it was mine
handmade, specially, for me. I'd have
saved it in a trunk, lined with lavender
for later, for my little girl.

Sometimes I remember that feeling
that *cornflower blue dress with tatting* feeling
the gladness that it was mine
the sadness that it was gone.
It is possible to feel that way without a blue dress
both glad and sad, though there be nothing
but a memory of my tatted blue cloud.

Time in a tisket

It rained on the gardener while
Ella sang "a-tisket a-tasket"
what is a tisket, a tasket?
(she knew a basket
to fill with flowers
good things to eat)
words make sense in song
like seeing blue even though
there is none in a blue-jay.

She was waiting
in the rain and waiting.

Time, that fair-weather friend
dashes by under the sun
stands still in the fog
waits in the rain
for something else
to arrive

like seeds popping up
at peril of being
a crow's breakfast.

Scare-away line worries crows
its iridescence torments them
shimmering, catching sun's rays
drops of dew (perhaps)

feeling its relentless glimmer
its harmless high-pitched wail
crows flee, afraid of an innocent
glistening prismatic silver line
that cannot hurt them
only protects salad for growing.

Then she'd fill a basket
with plenty, with flowers
and a song.

It rained.
She waited.
Seeds grew.
Time passed.

City planners

Where is the city for lost hearts?
ones that made a mistake
    missed a chance
    tried to start fresh
    needed to say sorry.

How to get there from here?
surely there'll be a map
    old landmarks
    familiar directions
    detours marked.

Will there be streets with names?
places to remember
    Monday's school yard
    Friday's dance hall
    Sunday's forgiveness.

Can the road be found again?
memory kept its own pictures
    never go back
    everything is small
    nothing as before.

Who thought of such a place?
a city for lost hearts
    peculiar notion
    curious memory
    oblivion observed.

Sandstone

I turn over sandstones
to look for salamanders

walking the mellow
untravelled way today
I feel light as an armload of barley
blowing in a summer wind

I do not feel like a poem

found a charcoal drawing
a horizon
pictured with a line of sombre spruce
to mark the place where contentment
came at sunset

a bracken fungus grew up
ready for taking
except I was not strong enough
to lift that treasure

not I

it told a bold and beautiful
story of dying on a solitary tree

I think
someone will help me
bring home
the bracken fungus

I *am* able to turn over sandstones
and sometimes find salamanders

Worms

Spring opens winter shutters
sun warms, hangs long in the sky
the earth softens
cultivated by worms
labouring at instinct's
particular profession
below, where we cannot go.

Oh worm! We go down
into our own deep
far from the light
where ego's dangerous desires
create terror for
woman––child––old innocents.

On foot in our own deep
beguiled by monstrous mammon
we finally appear
shrivelled
unrecognizable
barren

while the worms carry on
in perfect harmony
below, where we cannot go.

The *Fall of Rome* encore

Mother used to say, "The world is going to hell in a hand-basket." Too true. Now I see a culture-war decline resembling fall-of-Rome chaos: loss of polite manners; corrosion of language to crudeness; fashion's acceptance of indecency; violence abounding in movies, games, tv, comics, books, schoolyards, sports, and most tragically— relationships. The ever-growing list of our discomfiting descent.

Damning any form of our despair makes no sense, since we are all to blame—even complacent silence is a form of acquiescence. Who shall cast the first stone? In every human endeavour, in every moment, there are only two choices available—choose life or choose death. The ultimate choosing life is giving birth; the ultimate choosing death is murder. Everyday 'choosing life' is a smile given a stranger, a hungry person fed, a lost animal returned, a worried soul comforted, a birthday celebrated, a cut bandaged, a hug shared. Everyday 'choosing death' is a frown to the world, an untruth spread in gossip, a be-loved shunned, a laugh over put-down humour, a cruel comment unchallenged, language fouled, forgiveness withheld.

We do go down. Like worms, but not like worms.

White as a whale

A cloud floated by
then vanished
a waft of ballet chiffon
high, untouchable white
cumulus nimbus gone

winter's snowy, immaculate palette—
astonished itself.
Is white like death
cold frozen or
like seeing with
bracing clarity?
(winter white for contemplation)

Green feels safer.
No one ever froze to death in green.

White flowers shine in moonlight
daisy blossoms light
the garden path at midnight
small perfect spheres, glowing.

An albino whale
prized, hunted, hated to death
feared, triumphed, followed
beneath dark waters
where only the moon
would catch his motion.

The albino, the forerunner
mistook as aberration.

Wolfy

Looking beyond death in B minor,
his Lachrymosa wept with joy.
The end was near, before the finish.
As if it mattered.
He had seen through the veil
countless times and could
not prevent heaven's notes arriving
from early beginning, to early end.

Wrinkled gold

A bowl of wrinkled gold quince
majesty held in mellow perfume
sustained till the very end
while everything else
tempting
perished.

IV. Whither are we bound

Now and then, alone

Morning hangs with fog on meadow
where certain cherished fancies brim with hope,
til sunup lifts the fog, a haze of mist, sweet
then gone, with no sufficient interlope
of yearning beneath fragments of lonesome
courage, never quite spoken, this ration
of grace, a modest fortune —lush, fulsome—
emerges in a privilege of secret compassion
for a dream unshared, uncheered, unseen,
rooted only inside my own heart, where
tended things grow and flower and even
weeds are offered a chance to glory in a bouquet,
yet never follow that eclipsed desire
to go where feet have wings and then, retire.

Cadence

Early winter landscape in stubble
brindle grass with snow drifting
    and wind
a marriage of the remnants of November
with the prospect of December's white mantle
in time for weighing the bare truth.

On the radio, three *Ave Maria's*, one after another.
Bruckner with too many inspirations for one *Ave*
all divine – the music, the thought, the inspiration,
    the wind.
Landscape and song combined
to devote a time for *petit deuil*

a *little mourning* for something lost
always a little something more
graciously, not all at once
    like wind.
Providence's rhythm for learning
if suffering is a song or a prayer.

Choristers called early for singing
in preparation for His arrival
on the darkest day of winter
    holy wind.
  "Balulalow, balulalow, balulalow...
and I sall rock Thee in my heart..."*

Cadence on holy wind.

"sall" being old English, here quoted from the motet
"Balulalow" by Marc Sirrett

Faraway

His token, a cruet filled
with flowering currant
pungent gold spice
scent of the faraway
mysterious East
or sweet perfume
for the simple here and now.

No food

There is not enough food
maise in Kitale
rice in Chongqing
chicken brains in Bouaké
seal blubber in Igloolik
tree grubs in LaRoija
latkeys in Boyarka
barely enough to go around.

Like the loaves and fishes
the bowl is passed, each one
given portion enough to live
to carry on and smile—
the bewildering part.
Where can it come from
joy in the middle of hunger?

All you can eat buffet
that's what the ad said.
All you can eat, how much is that?
Enough to feed a small country?
Enough to get sick?
Enough to forget
everything?

This is North America where
everyone is hungry
you can see it on our faces
starved in fact
round and full and starved.
Starved for joy
empty but so full.

It has been too long since
we have forgotten how
the loaves and fishes
filled the baskets
what that really meant
for the feeding of our joy.

Echo

An emptied space filled with an echo
the repetition of sound by reflection;
the obsequious imitator;
the apparatus for determining
the depth of the sea:
    air in diverse tone dances
    as deep as the bottom of the sea
    as empty as a wind whip in a hollow place
    that echoed without words
    when air repeated its nothingness.

Air relinquishes emptiness
to fire and water
a filling for the echo place
its void
    feverish and drenched
    ardent and immersed
    unable to withstand hot and wet

looks face to face upon fire and water worlds

forces the misadventure that
creates the echo in the first place.

Unless the fire had no intent but a warmth.
Unless the water had no thirst but an inspiration.
Unless the words had no dream but a bridge.

Glass sky

a full moon lights night clouds
a lantern overtaking obscurity
silver ambush rounding a grey day
unexpected
exotic

the recurring transformation is
creation's habit:
the tips of stars shine,
the edges of souls are faint

waiting
for the weathered memory
of a glass sky

Leaf paint

Trees adorned in the triumphs of sunrise and sunset
impossible colour with unassuming perfection
touched my thinking and my knowing
sorrow searching, joy brightening
longing heart and soul, with crowns of gold.

I felt drawn from one far edge of a painting to the other
my place, my country, my desire, my hope, my everything
leaf paint of red-fused-on-yellow transformed to orange
gold
or was it yellow-on-red, perplexing to fathom
how colours move to unimaginable heights, depths.

Red and yellow conjoined inside my soul
I've thought of it like that before
when lowliness of heart looked upon
my meagre knowing beside celestial mysteries
so quiet, filled my soul's banquet with sweetness
                    and drew me near.

Butterfly wind

While the bobolink sang
I stood near lilacs to capture
perfume—a June day so fragrant, serene—
and chanced to feel a butterfly wind
like a poem whispering on my cheek

butterfly wind
a moment, a flutter
in no hurry
long enough to leave a memory
then vanish, wings wafting

wind one can not hold
wind one can but know

is love like that?
impression, not seen but felt
ethereal, not adamant yet mighty

is love like that?
reaching, extending beyond
finding one to touch

is love like that?
a whisper song of no word
a sung canticle of every word

is love like that?
finding another, an other
then losing self in giving

is love like that?
honour rapture ardour bliss
conjoined with unaccustomed peace

It was a gift to find
the marks of love fly by
in a dulcet butterfly wind.

And still the bobolink sang.

Dry tears

If I could choose my imperfections
my heart would not be set
so near the surface
where its beat keeps time with
other hearts nearby.
Their pulse the gift of
abundant, seeing tears.

I wondered long about this
until a wise woman told me
tears are from the merciful.

And yet, I would set my heart
deep inside where all those beats
cannot reach, except one fine place
enough to hold the tears inside
no bother to any soul
while eyes with dry tears tell
the secret in my heart.

Quiet place

there is a quiet place
the cusp of daybreak
where breath expels
like calm petitions
in matin's litany

there is a hearth side
where logs burn red hot
and blue, the perfect flame
the cool, distant colour
in morning's responsory

there is a waking jewel
sun kindled illumination
days's primal offering
while sky, wakened holy
halts aurora's vigil

there is a simple prayer
ardent daily thanks
for morning's life begot
while thought, fire, light
converge in celebration

there is a perfect freedom
contained in morning's brow
princely mantle, light as air
the very thought of Thee
then thanks at eventide

Night heart

like silk woven strong as steel
mother-love bonds
never weary, never weaken
spun for life to hold
the essence of their hearts
in hers
buried treasure unburied
hopes hurts happiness
so in the darkness of the night
remembering each care twice
for them, for her
and having run the course
every breath taken or given
till at last, in ample time
they'll feel a mother-heart beat
when they spin their own
silken threads of silver love

Teresa of Avila

Seven beads that glow in the dark
strung on midnight blue ribbon
with knots between, a separation.
Seven little full moons hanging
    with seven longings
that could only be seen
    along the journey from
    darkness to the light.

The first bead was for waiting
    the second for listening
    the third for asking
    the fourth for entering
    the fifth for desiring
    the sixth for giving
    the seventh for thanking.

That she may walk with a perfect heart.
That she may walk with a perfect heart
before Thee now and ever more.

Quinquagesima

Behold Quinquagesima
a myriad of interior moments

meticulous looking forward
backward, into the centre

being winter, always
a time of no honey bees

the time of ice petals
though apple blossoms

lurk in hearts for a honey bee's
tiny feet to stop where

they won't paralyse
as souls recall being

children of love
no trembling burden

where everything's given
for our need and our offering.

Quinquagesima.

Lark

Music filled a space with
importuning strings,
inviting the graceful delicate
wings of an ascending lark
soft, pale, tentative grey
sweet with air, uplifting
head held so
body light with air.

Is that what we mean:
light as a feather?
I stopped to listen.
But it rained
petals without light
exchanged their wonder,
lucid to ambiguous.

Rain by gravity descending
steals flight away.
A lark requires empty air
it cannot share its wings
with rain
to rise, to soar.

Burdened too,
the lark must wait
until a void makes way
for lifting up
and up and up.

It isn't what it has but
what it does not have.
It isn't what it does but
what it does not do.

Window ash

Ash made of
salt from the sea
soil from the land
squall-etched on the pane
like transgressions on my soul.

The winter air is clean as clean
blue sky, saffron sun, white snow
icicles
and chilling wind to freeze
a God-child heart.
And no view through the window.

A perpetually clouded sash
without water to wash the ash from my window.

The ice grows hour by hour.
Warmth is here by the fire
the inside of contemplation
where salt and sand exact their price
scratching the edges off
what I have done, but ought not to do,
what I ought to do, but have not done.

I fall through window ash
while love repeats its song
of limitless gift.
So hard.
Storms well up in my soul.
Giving up myself is hard.

Open the stove—sparks flame.
Open the soul—love sparks.

If I had a river

If I had the sun or the moon, I'd give it you.
If I had a star or a cloud, I'd give it you.
If I had a river, I'd give it you
    or a rose, or a rainbow
    a poem, a dream, or a song, I'd give it you.

My all to give.
You gave me yours.

Wings

Last night I dreamt of wings
several kinds to take me places
      wings
        always on high

just good to know
        in the shelter of
        which ones

I am flying.

Banquet

I entered the expanse
in a dream and a prayer,
an ivory marble dome
with *kyrie eleison* singing,

and listening, was invited
to supper with Love,
unable to speak,
heart pounding.

Old perfect poem

If I have found the perfect poem
with words that touch my heart
sufficient, what more to write?

Here & now, words struggle
Mocked and scorned since
"lol", "omg", "i luv u" suffice.

Written word has shrunk to fit a 4.5 inch screen.
Turn over or around—4.5 is enough.
Spelling, penmanship, paper and pen? No.

A perfect poem was written by a
gentle soul in 1400, by his hand
long hand. Remember?

A poet, in no hurry.
It takes time to be given a poem.
A perfect poem.

I carry this poem in my heart
implanted in myocyte cells
the rhythm makers of the heart.

Be quiet. Listen. Wait. Love will find you.
It will seek your soul and burn
till ardour kindles love within you.

Acknowledgments

Looking about one's small spot in the world and capturing what that is all about in poems can feel like a futile activity. Yet something happens when poems are shared because their matter, yet breathing, is completed in the mind and heart of the reader. Since I am seeing these poems published at a rather advanced point in my life, my gracious thanks to Terrilee Bulger and Acorn Press for taking a chance on me. It is the small presses which do the utmost in telling the stories of local culture and in vital ways, no matter the risk.

A competent editor makes a book a finer version of itself. I am deeply indebted to Dianne Hicks Morrow for her incomparable contribution to *the whither poems*. Her editing experience and writing talents taught me much.

Carrying on in what is a solitary activity requires some nudging. Endless thanks to David Aurandt who was a relentless prodder in this role. Some people just don't let one give up. David didn't.

Helen Steinberg and I have had a lifetime of letter writing in the 'habit of being' way, à la Flannery O'Connor, which has been a joy and a sustaining blessing in my life. Helen is much funnier.

Hugh MacDonald and Carolyn Duffy Ledwell and I were students together at St. Dunstan's University in the 1960s. It was a vibrant and momentous time. Thank you for being such willing and insightful readers.

To my husband, Michael and to Gethin & Meg, Steven, Crispin, Samuel, Cecily & Shaun, Ruby, Joseph, Eric & Lisa, Isaac, Frances, John I can hardly thank you enough for insuring I have not had a boring day in these past 47+ years. I look forward to the trend continuing.... well, maybe slower.